BREAKING FREE FROM THE CHAINS OF OVERTHINKING

Unleashing Your Mind From The Grip Of Anxiety And Doubt

By

Paul Ernest

Paul Ernest

INTRODUCTION

THE PERVASIVE EFFECT OF OVERTHINKING IN CONTEMPORARY LIFE

The sensation of overthinking has become a pervasive and oppressive force in our lives in an era of nonstop information, never-ending diversions, and ever-increasing demands. We become caught up in a never-ending web of ideas, analyzing the past, fretting about the future, and dwelling on the details of the present. These constant thought patterns not only make it difficult for us to think clearly, but they also deplete our mental and emotional energy, leaving us feeling agitated, nervous, and exhausted.

Ernest Paul, a distinguished author and a recognized authority on mental well-being, brings you "Breaking Free from the Chains of Overthinking" - a comprehensive exploration of this modern affliction and a road map to liberation. With a wealth of knowledge and a profound understanding of the human psyche, Paul leads readers on a trans-formative journey toward regaining control over their minds and lives.

The book begins by dissecting the intricate web of overthinking, peeling back the layers to reveal the root causes of this relentless habit. Paul delves into the insidious connection between overthinking and anxiety, perfectionism, and past trauma, helping readers understand how these factors feed the overactive mind.

As the journey unfolds, the book exposes the far-reaching consequences of overthinking. It is a silent saboteur that disrupts our decision-making processes, sabotages our relationships, and even manifests in physical health issues. Readers will gain insight into the undeniable impact of this mental trap on their lives.

However, this book offers more than just an awareness of overthinking; it also serves as a practical manual for escaping its control. Paul arms readers with a toolkit of methods to calm the racing mind, lessen stress, and live with newly discovered clarity and confidence. Readers who delve into the worlds of mindfulness, meditation, and self-compassion will learn practical strategies for calming the onslaught of ideas and emerging as confident, self-aware people.

Throughout the journey, the book offers practical exercises to unlock creative potential, enhance emotional intelligence, and build resilience. From improving sleep patterns to parenting with confidence and navigating professional life with ease, readers will find a holistic approach to liberating themselves from the chains of overthinking.

"Breaking Free from the Chains of Overthinking" by Ernest Paul is an inspiring manual that equips readers to take charge of their mental selves. Readers will discover the secrets of unlocking tranquility, seizing chances, and rekindling their enthusiasm for life in these pages. Start now on your trans-formative road to mental emancipation and don't allow overthinking hold you back.

CHAPTER 0NE

1. THE OVERTHINKING EPIDEMIC

Over overthinking a single concept or group of thoughts repeatedly and intensely to the point that it interferes with daily functioning and general well-being is known as overthinking. It entails either an anxious obsession with future worries, known as worrying or an obsessive focus on previous occurrences, a behavior known as rumination. Over-analyzing may have a severe impact on one's mental health, encourage perfectionist tendencies, and start a vicious cycle of negative ideas. Overthinking is more prone to happen to those with anxiety problems. It is generally caused by a propensity to worry excessively, and frequently about things that are out of one's control. It can eventually lead to the emergence of anxiety disorders and melancholy. Maintaining mental and emotional wellness requires awareness of these tendencies and using techniques to address and regulate overthinking.

Acknowledging its Frequency

Recognizing a phenomenon's or problem's frequency within a certain environment or civilization is referred to as "recognizing the prevalence" or "becoming aware of the prevalence." It entails realizing that a certain issue, habit, or disease is widespread and has a substantial impact on a lot of individuals.

In the context of the introduction to "Breaking Free from the Chains of Overthinking," "recognizing the prevalence" would involve acknowledging that overthinking is not an isolated or uncommon problem. It is something that many individuals grapple with, and it is a pervasive issue in today's society.

The book tries to emphasize that overthinking is a common and shared difficulty and that readers are not alone in their battle by acknowledging its ubiquity. It might be comforting to know that others have had similar experiences as one's own since it makes one feel less alone in their struggles. Additionally, it prepares readers for what the book seeks to achieve, which is to face the issue collectively and look for ideas to solve it.

The Emotional and Mental Cost

"The Psychological and Emotional Toll" emphasizes the significant weight that overthinking causes on a person's mental and emotional well being. Stress is a common trigger for overthinking, which can appear as a pattern of unceasing negative rumination in which ideas become consuming and persistent. This negative mental habit has a negative impact on one's emotional state, increasing tension, worry, and occasionally even depression.

If left untreated, overthinking could turn into a regular habit. It not only has an effect on emotional well-being but also puts one's physical and mental health at danger. Overthinking, according to studies, can have a number of detrimental effects, including:

- **Elevated Blood Pressure:** Stress from overthinking might result in high blood pressure. Stress can lead to poor coping behaviors like smoking and binge drinking, which can be harmful to cardiovascular health.

- **Sleep Disturbances:** Overthinking often causes insomnia or poor-quality sleep. This results in fatigue, reduced productivity, and an increased likelihood of weight gain due to overeating.

- **Appetite Suppression:** Overthinking can disrupt normal hunger signals, causing a loss of appetite. Alternatively, it may lead to overeating, both of which can be detrimental to health.

- **Brain Impact:** Overthinking can alter brain structure and connectivity, contributing to mood disorders such as anxiety, stress, and depression. It can impair focus, problem-solving, and decision-making abilities.

- **Digestive Issues:** The stress induced by overthinking affects the digestive system by reducing blood flow and oxygen supply to the stomach. This can result in gastrointestinal problems like inflammatory bowel disease (IBD) and irritable bowel syndrome (IBS).

- **Weakened Immune System:**

The stress hormone cortisol, which damages the immune system, is released when someone overthinks. Allergies, infections, and illnesses are all made more likely as a result.

The first step in escaping the grip of overthinking is realizing the psychological and emotional costs it imposes. This book provides advice and techniques to assist people in regaining control over their thoughts, lowering their stress levels, and regaining their emotional and mental well-being.

CHAPTER TWO

1. THE EFFECT OF MAKING DECISIONS

The book tries to emphasize that overthinking is a comm on and shared difficulty and that readers are not alone in t heir battle by acknowledging its ubiquity.

It might be comforting to know that others have had simil ar experiences as one's own since it makes one feel less a lone in their struggles.

Additionally, it prepares readers for what the book seeks to achieve, which is to face the issue collectively and loo k for ideas to solve it.The book tries to emphasize that ov erthinking is a common and shared difficulty and that rea ders are not alone in their battle by acknowledging its ubi quity.

It might be comforting to know that others have had simil ar experiences as one's own since it makes one feel less a lone in their struggles.

Additionally, it prepares readers for what the book seeks

to achieve, which is to face the issue collectively and loo
k for ideas to solve it.

"The analysis paralysis effect"

Within the intricate web of overthinking, one particular snare is the paralyzing effect of analysis. It's a trap many fall into, mistakenly believing that relentless scrutiny of decisions is a sign of diligence and intelligence. In this chapter, we will unravel the intricacies of analysis paralysis and its role in overthinking, offering a path to liberation through effective decision-making techniques.

Understanding the Perils of Analysis Paralysis

Complex phenomenon known as "analysis paralysis" causes people to become mired in a never-ending loop of deliberation. It frequently passes for caution and thoroughness, with individuals thinking that the more they consider a choice, the better. But nothing could be farther from the truth than this. Analysis paralysis really operates as a sort of procrastination, when the tendency to overthink becomes a barrier to acting. This section acts as a wake-up call to the harmful nature of analytical paralysis, illuminating its ability to impede advancement and limit the achievement of improved results. It enables readers to see how, far from being a sign of wisdom, overthinking frequently results in inefficient decision-making and immobility.

Breaking Free from Analysis Paralysis

The appropriate tactics can help you escape the grip of analytical paralysis, which is not an easy task. The key idea of categorizing analytical paralysis as a type of procrastination is introduced to readers in this section. People might start along the path to emancipation by learning that ineffective decision-making and action are frequently hampered by excessive analysis. The trick is to go from a continual state of analysis to one of deliberate, certain action. In order to break the pattern of overthinking, this chapter offers readers useful strategies and tactics that will enable them to make decisions quickly and confidently.

The Balance Between Analysis and Action

This chapter's main idea is around the skill of finding a balance between thorough analysis and determined action. Overthinking frequently traps people in a frustrating loop of uncertainty, making it difficult to go forward. This section looks at how to strike a balance between the level of study required to make a choice and the activity needed to carry it out successfully. The chapter stresses how overthinking may become a paralyzing trap and provides helpful techniques to escape it. Readers may make more effective and confident decisions by grasping this balance.

2. TIMELY DECISION-MAKING

This section places a spotlight on the importance of making decisions promptly, especially in critical areas like healthcare and education. Delaying decisions can result in a multitude of negative consequences. The section underlines the significance of acting swiftly rather than succumbing to the allure of prolonged contemplation. Readers will gain insight into the real-world implications of procrastination and the urgency of overcoming it. The message is clear: timely decision-making is a key aspect of breaking free from analysis paralysis, enabling individuals to seize opportunities and align their choices with their goals and priorities.

STRATEGIES FOR BREAKING FREE

To break free from analysis paralysis, it's crucial to set deadlines for decisions and learn to take calculated risks. Adopting a growth mindset is also important;

understanding that mistakes are opportunities for learning can boost confidence in decision-making. Building self-trust through small, incremental choices is another effective strategy.

By understanding these nuances of overthinking, individuals can begin the journey to breaking free from these patterns, gaining greater control over their thought processes, and ultimately making more confident and timely decisions.

CHAPTER 3

1. THE COGNITIVE PROCESS OF OVERTHINKING

Endless Reflection

A common symptom of overthinking is endless reflection, in which people find themselves constantly going over previous encounters, exchanges, or choices. Over-thinkers may analyze prior incidents or probe each subtlety of a previous discussion, but this unrelenting mental rumination frequently results in no conclusion. They could also reflect on embarrassing, repentant, or guilty events. Key understandings of eternal contemplation include:

The Nature of Endless Reflection

Over thinkers can't easily let go of past events or experiences. This process of replaying and analyzing past situations can be time-consuming and emotionally draining.

2. IMPACT ON MENTAL WELL-BEING

Endless reflection takes a toll on mental well-being. It often leads to heightened levels of stress, anxiety, and emotional distress. Over-thinkers may experience sleep disturbances as their minds remain active, replaying past events late into the night.

Strategies for Breaking Free

Over-thinkers are advised to establish limits for ruminating in order to relieve themselves from endless pondering. While realizing that not everything can be rectified or made perfect, they should try to put an end to the events of the past. For this cycle to be broken, attention must be shifted to the present and future. It may be beneficial to use strategies like journaling, mindfulness, and cognitive behavioral therapy.

3. EXAGGERATED WORRY

Exaggerated worry is a manifestation of overthinking that involves taking common concerns and magnifying them into overwhelming anxieties. Over-thinkers often anticipate worst-case scenarios and tend to overestimate potential negative outcomes. The key insights into exaggerated worry include:

Understanding Exaggerated Worry

Overthinking amplifies everyday concerns due to a desire for absolute control or a fear of the unknown. It transforms minor worries into debilitating anxieties, often leading to a perpetual state of stress.

Impact on Mental Health

Exaggerated worry is closely linked to heightened stress and anxiety. Over-thinkers may constantly feel on edge, leading to physical symptoms like headaches and tension. It can negatively impact overall mental well-being, potentially contributing to conditions like generalized anxiety disorder.

Coping Strategies

Understanding the difference between reasonable and irrational anxieties is a necessary step in overcoming excessive anxiety. Deep breathing and other mindfulness techniques, such as meditation, can assist people in taking control of their racing thoughts. Re-framing negative thinking patterns is one cognitive-behavioral method that can help over-thinkers alter how they perceive and react to concern.

CHAPTER 4
CAUSES OF THE OVERTHINKING

1. The Effects of Perfectionism

Perfectionism, or the unrelenting quest of feeling, looking, and being flawless, is a characteristic that is frequently praised by society as admirable. It's important to understand, though, that striving for perfection can have both advantages and disadvantages, as covered in "Breaking Free from the Chains of Overthinking."

❖ The Signs of Perfectionism

Recognizing perfectionism often starts with understanding the signs that indicate its presence. As previously highlighted, these signs include:

Feeling Extremely Down or Depressed When You Fail

Perfectionists invest their self-worth in their achievements. When they fall short or make a mistake, they experience deep sadness or even depression. Their sense of self becomes intricately tied to their successes, making any setback feel like a personal failure.

Constantly Thinking That Your Work Is Never Good Enough

Perfectionists are rarely content with their work. They perpetually believe that their efforts are inadequate. This unending self-critique leads to a cycle of striving for an unattainable standard of perfection and frustration when it remains out of reach.

Hindrance to Progress by Focusing on Failures

Perfectionism often directs attention to what went wrong rather than acknowledging achievements. Perfectionists become preoccupied with their missteps and shortcomings, which can hinder progress by sapping motivation and self-confidence. Rather than celebrating their successes, they are more likely to dwell on their perceived inadequacies.

Defensiveness When Errors Are Pointed Out

Perfectionism can show up as defensiveness in response to criticism or mistakes pointed out by others. Any criticism is frequently interpreted as a personal jab at their skill. This defensiveness may strain relationships in both the personal and professional spheres by impeding learning from mistakes and personal progress.

Belief That Asking for Help Is a Sign of Weakness

Perfectionists frequently think that asking for assistance is a sign of weakness or incapacity. They frequently believe they are autonomous and capable of managing everything. As a result of carrying an excessive load alone and without assistance from others, this way of thinking can cause stress and burnout.

THE EFFECTS OF PERFECTIONISM

Perfectionism carries profound effects, and understanding its dual nature is crucial for managing it effectively.

Positive Aspects

At its core, perfectionism can be a driving force for achievement and personal growth. When channeled constructively, it motivates individuals to set high standards, pursue excellence, and continuously challenge themselves to improve. It underlies remarkable accomplishments in various domains, from art and science to athletics and business.

Negative Effects

the pursuit of perfection can easily transform into a relentless tormentor. The potential negative effects include:

- **Extreme Emotional Reactions to Failure:** Perfectionists often tie their self-worth to their achievements, leading to deep sadness or even depression when they fall short.

- **Chronic Dissatisfaction with One's Work:** Perfectionists are rarely satisfied with their own work, perpetually believing it falls short.

- **Hindrance to Progress:** Perfectionism can hinder progress by sapping motivation and self-confidence, as individuals become preoccupied with their perceived inadequacies.

- **Defensiveness:** It can lead to defensiveness when others offer critiques, hampering personal growth and straining relationships.

- **Reluctance to Seek Help:** finally, perfectionism can be a potent source of motivation and personal growth, but it can also lead to emotional distress, chronic dissatisfaction, hindered progress, defensiveness, and reluctance to seek help. Recognizing these effects is the first step in managing perfectionism to ensure it remains a driving force for achievement rather than a source of distress.

2.   TRAUMA AND OVERTHINKING

"Freedom from the Chains of the Past"

The intersection of past trauma and overthinking is a complex and profound aspect of the human psyche. It's a topic that explores the intricate relationship between past experiences, their lingering effects on our mental and emotional well-being, and how these experiences can lead to a pattern of overthinking. Within the pages of "Breaking Free from the Chains of Overthinking," this subject emerges as a critical point of exploration, shedding light on the challenges individuals face when they are unable to free themselves from the shackles of their past.

Understanding Past Trauma: Past trauma, often referred to as emotional or psychological trauma, encompasses experiences that overwhelm an individual's ability to cope, leaving a lasting impact on their mental and emotional state. Traumatic events can vary widely, ranging from physical or emotional abuse, accidents, loss of a loved one, or natural disasters to experiences like bullying, neglect, or witnessing violence.

Trauma often leaves individuals with a deep sense of vulnerability and distress, and its effects can manifest in many ways. Some individuals may develop post-traumatic stress disorder (PTSD), while others might experience persistent anxiety, depression, or even a sense of disconnection from themselves and the world.

The Lingering Effects of Trauma: One of the primary reasons past trauma is intertwined with overthinking is the enduring effects it has on an individual's mental and emotional well-being. Trauma survivors frequently find themselves haunted by intrusive memories, nightmares, and a heightened state of alertness, known as hyper arousal. These symptoms often lead to a constant state of hyper-vigilance, where the individual is always on the lookout for potential threats, whether real or perceived.

The mental and emotional scars of trauma can significantly affect one's self-esteem and sense of self-worth. Survivors may struggle with feelings of guilt, shame, or even a sense of detachment from their own emotions. These unresolved emotions become fertile ground for overthinking, as the individual attempts to make sense of their traumatic experiences and find a way to heal.

The Cycle of Overthinking and Trauma: Overthinking can be both a response to past trauma and a perpetuator of its effects. Trauma survivors often engage in overthinking as a coping mechanism. They ruminate on the traumatic event, attempting to process it and find a way to prevent such an experience from happening again. This constant mental rehashing can lead to an unending cycle of rumination, guilt, and self-blame.

Moreover, overthinking in the context of past trauma can manifest as excessive worry about future events. Trauma survivors may develop a heightened sensitivity to potential threats, leading to a constant state of "what if" thinking. They become preoccupied with anticipating danger, which can lead to chronic stress and anxiety.

The Impact on Daily Life: The intersection of past trauma and overthinking can significantly impact an individual's daily life. It often leads to a heightened sense of vigilance and anxiety, making it challenging to relax or experience moments of peace. Trauma survivors might avoid situations or triggers that remind them of their traumatic experiences, which can limit their life experiences and opportunities for growth.

In relationships, trauma-related overthinking can lead to difficulties in trust and emotional intimacy. The fear of being vulnerable can lead to a sense of isolation and an inability to connect with others on a deep level.

Furthermore, overthinking can erode self-confidence and hinder personal and professional growth.

Breaking Free from the Chains: The book "Breaking Free from the Chains of Overthinking" explores the methods and approaches people may use to end the overthinking cycle that is caused by traumatic experiences in the past. It highlights how crucial it is to get professional assistance when coping with trauma and obsessive thinking since therapy and counseling may offer a secure setting for examining and working through these difficult feelings.

Recognizing the effects of trauma and accepting that overthinking is a normal reaction to such situations are crucial first steps toward ending this cycle. People are able to cease criticizing themselves for their ideas and feelings when they practice self-compassion.

The Journey Towards Healing: The intersection of past trauma and overthinking is a challenging terrain to navigate. Trauma survivors often find themselves caught in a relentless cycle of rehashing the past and worrying about the future. However, with the right support, strategies, and a willingness to embark on the journey toward healing, it is possible to break free from the shackles of overthinking.

The book "Breaking Free from the Chains of Overthinking" offers a comprehensive guide for individuals seeking to confront and conquer their overthinking tendencies, especially when rooted in past trauma. By recognizing the profound impact of past trauma on overthinking and employing strategies to address it, individuals can embark on a path toward healing, resilience, and a brighter future.

Key Note:

Overthinking and prior trauma are closely related, which can start a vicious cycle that negatively impacts a person's mental and emotional health. Acknowledging this link and utilizing techniques to release oneself from the constraints of the past is an essential first step toward recovery and personal development. The book is a great tool for anybody trying to get over the difficulties of overthinking in the wake of tragedy. It provides direction and encouragement

2. THE IMPACT OF SOCIAL AND ENVIRONMENTAL FACTORS ON ANXIETY

Social and environmental variables, especially in relation to anxiety, are major determinants of our mental and emotional health in the fast-paced, connected world we live in today. By thoroughly examining these elements, the book "Breaking Free from the Chains of Overthinking" illuminates the intricate network of outside pressures and how they affect people's lives. This thorough investigation is an invaluable tool for comprehending, negotiating, and eventually conquering the difficulties brought about by these elements.

Societal Pressures: Our society exerts significant pressure on individuals to conform to certain standards of success, appearance, and behavior. This constant comparison to societal norms can lead to anxiety as people strive to meet these often unrealistic expectations.

The book delves into how societal pressures, such as the pursuit of a perfect body, a high-paying job, or a picture-perfect family life, can foster anxiety. It emphasizes the importance of recognizing that these standards are often unattainable or not reflective of one's true desires, allowing readers to break free from the anxiety induced by societal expectations.

Economic Instability: Economic uncertainty and financial stress can be potent triggers for anxiety. Individuals facing job insecurity, mounting debt, or the fear of financial ruin are particularly vulnerable to anxiety disorders.

"Breaking Free from the Chains of Overthinking" addresses the impact of economic instability on mental well-being. It provides practical strategies for managing financial stress and making informed decisions in turbulent economic times, thus alleviating anxiety associated with financial concerns.

Rapid-Paced Modern Life: The hustle and bustle of modern life, characterized by its breakneck speed, information overload, and the incessant demands of technology, contribute significantly to heightened anxiety levels. The book acknowledges these factors and offers guidance on how to create a balanced and fulfilling life in a rapidly changing world.

It encourages readers to embrace mindfulness and find ways to disconnect from the constant barrage of information, providing a path to inner peace in a world that often feels chaotic and overwhelming.

Social Isolation: Loneliness and social isolation are well-established factors in anxiety and depression. "Breaking Free from the Chains of Overthinking" addresses the challenges of social disconnection in the digital age and offers strategies for building meaningful connections and combating isolation-induced anxiety.

Environmental Concerns: Anxiety related to environmental issues, such as climate change and natural disasters, is on the rise. The book discusses the psychological toll of environmental concerns and provides insights into managing Eco-anxiety through a combination of individual and collective actions.

Work-Life Imbalance: The blurred boundaries between work and personal life, along with the pressures of being constantly available through technology, contribute to work-related anxiety. The book explores strategies for achieving a healthy work-life balance, setting boundaries, and preventing work-related stress from seeping into one's personal life.

Discrimination and Social Injustice: The book also delves into the anxiety associated with discrimination, prejudice, and social injustice. It discusses how these issues can impact mental health and offers guidance on resilience, self-care, and advocating for change.

Key Note:

"Breaking Free from the Chains of Overthinking" essentially offers a thorough analysis of the ways in which social and environmental variables can exacerbate anxiety. In the face of the complicated problems of the modern world, it equips readers with the information and techniques necessary to negotiate these outside influences, lessen their impact, and finally attain inner peace and mental well-being.

CHAPTER 5

OVERTHINKING AND RELATIONSHIPS
1. COMMUNICATION STRESS

Relationships that are flourishing and healthy depend on communication. But it may also be a major cause of tension and worry, which can result in miscommunication, arguments, and over-analyzing. "Breaking Free from the Chains of Overthinking" discusses how communication stress may affect many facets of our daily life in the context of relationships and provides advice and techniques to help us get through these difficulties.

Understanding the Dynamics

The book recognizes that communication stress in relationships can stem from various factors, including fear of judgment, past negative experiences, difficulty in expressing emotions, or unresolved conflicts. It delves into the intricacies of these dynamics, helping readers identify and understand the root causes of their communication stress within the context of their relationships.

IMPACT ON RELATIONSHIPS

Stress in communication may have a big influence on relationships and health. Miscommunication, erroneous impressions, and emotional distance are typically the outcomes. For instance, ineffective communication can cause arguments, hurt feelings, and a decline in trust in romantic relationships. It might make friends uncomfortable or feel detached. It might lead to heated discussions and unresolved issues in family bonds.

The book focuses on how communication stress can initiate an overthinking loop in a relationship. People may begin to worry about future interactions, mentally relive past exchanges, and obsess on past interactions. This overanalyzing, which may be emotionally and mentally draining, can have a detrimental effect on the quality of a relationship.

STRATEGIES FOR MANAGING COMMUNICATION STRESS IN RELATIONSHIPS

"Breaking Free from the Chains of Overthinking" equips readers with strategies to manage and overcome communication stress within their relationships:

Active Listening: The book highlights the importance of active listening as a fundamental component of effective communication. It offers guidance on how to truly hear and understand what the other person is saying, reducing the likelihood of misunderstandings.

Empathy: Empathy is a critical skill for building and maintaining healthy relationships. The book provides practical advice on how to empathize with the thoughts and emotions of your partner, friend, or family member, fostering a sense of connection and emotional support.

Assertiveness: In many relationships, individuals struggle with assertiveness, often avoiding open and honest communication due to fear of conflict or confrontation. The book offers techniques for assertive communication, allowing individuals to express their needs and concerns without aggression or passivity.

Conflict Resolution: Conflict is a natural part of any relationship. The book introduces conflict resolution skills, teaching readers how to address disagreements in a healthy and constructive manner. By resolving conflicts effectively, individuals can reduce communication stress in relationships.

Mindfulness in Relationships: Mindfulness techniques are tailored to improve communication within relationships. Practicing mindfulness can help individuals stay present during interactions, reducing overthinking and anxiety about past or future conversations.

Self-Reflection and Self-Compassion: The book encourages self-reflection to better understand one's communication patterns and anxieties within relationships. It also promotes self-compassion, allowing individuals to be kinder to themselves and reduce self-blame when they make communication mistakes.

Real-Life Scenarios and Exercises

To help readers apply these strategies directly to their relationships, "Breaking Free from the Chains of Overthinking" incorporates real-life examples and practical exercises. These exercises provide opportunities for hands-on learning and foster a deeper understanding of how to manage and overcome communication stress within the context of personal relationships.

Key Note:

One complicated and important part of our personal life is the tension that comes with communicating in relationships. In addition to acknowledging the existence and effects of communication stress, the book offers readers insightful advice and useful management techniques. Through addressing this important relationship communication issue, the book enables readers to improve their interpersonal relationships, lessen worry and over-analyzing, and create happier, more satisfying partnerships.

2. OVERTHINKING IN PERSONAL RELATIONSHIPS

Our emotional health and sense of belonging to the world are fundamentally based on our interpersonal relationships. Whether they be familial ties, romantic partnerships, or friendships, these interactions give us solace, encouragement, and a feeling of community. Even though they may be lovely and rewarding, personal connections are not without difficulties. Overanalyzing is a major obstacle that frequently impedes personal interactions.

Overthinking in personal relationships refers to the persistent and excessive contemplation of various aspects of a relationship. It is the tendency to analyze every interaction, every word, and every gesture, seeking hidden meanings or potential pitfalls that may not even exist. While some degree of reflection is a normal part of maintaining healthy relationships, overthinking takes this to an extreme. It can lead to a cascade of anxiety, misunderstandings, and emotional distance.

THE COMPLEX NATURE OF OVERTHINKING IN PERSONAL RELATIONSHIPS

Overthinking in personal relationships can manifest in various ways. It often starts innocently, perhaps with a simple miscommunication or a perceived slight. The individual begins to mull over the situation, dissecting it from multiple angles, and attempting to unravel the motivations and intentions of their partner, friend, or family member. This process can quickly spiral into a relentless cycle of rumination.

One common manifestation of overthinking in personal relationships is excessive worry about the future. Individuals may become preoccupied with concerns about where the relationship is headed, whether their partner truly loves them, or if they are compatible in the long term. This future-focused overthinking can lead to a constant state of unease and apprehension.

Additionally, overthinking often involves dwelling on the past. Past arguments, misunderstandings, or perceived betrayals become fodder for relentless rumination. Individuals may replay these moments in their minds, analyzing what they could have said or done differently, and stewing in regret.

Another sign of overthinking is a constant quest for confirmation. Overthinkers may urge their partners to validate their love or commitment, which can be a source of ongoing anxiety. Both sides may get weary and frustrated with this conduct, which may strain the bond even more.

The Root Causes of Overthinking in Personal Relationships

To address overthinking in personal relationships, it's essential to understand the root causes. Several factors can contribute to this tendency:

Insecurity: Insecurity is a common driver of overthinking in relationships. Individuals who doubt their self-worth or fear abandonment may be more prone to over-analyze every aspect of their relationship, searching for proof of their partner's affection and commitment.

Past Trauma: Past traumas, such as previous abusive relationships or a history of family conflicts, can create a heightened state of alertness in new relationships. Individuals who have experienced trauma may be more vigilant for signs of potential harm, leading to overthinking.

Attachment Styles: Attachment theory suggests that our early attachment experiences shape our adult relationships. Those with anxious attachment styles may be more prone to overthinking and seeking constant reassurance in their relationships.

Perfectionism: Perfectionists tend to set unrealistically high standards for themselves and their relationships. When these standards are not met, they may engage in overthinking, trying to identify what went wrong and how to fix it.

Fear of Vulnerability: Some individuals fear vulnerability and emotional intimacy. Overthinking can serve as a defense mechanism, keeping their partner at arm's length to protect themselves from potential emotional pain.

Impact on Personal Relationships

The consequences of overthinking in personal relationships can be profound. While the individual may believe they are protecting the relationship or preventing harm, the opposite often occurs. The constant questioning, seeking of reassurance, and analysis can lead to significant stress and strain on the relationship.

Misunderstandings: Overthinking can lead to misunderstandings. The overthinker may read too much into a simple statement or action, misinterpreting their partner's intentions. This can result in unnecessary arguments and hurt feelings.

Emotional Distance: Overthinking can create emotional distance in a relationship. The constant need for reassurance and validation can be exhausting for the partner, leading them to withdraw emotionally.

Anxiety: Overthinking is a significant source of anxiety in personal relationships. The individual may be in a constant state of worry, fearing the loss of the relationship or potential future conflicts.

Communication Breakdown: Overthinking can hinder effective communication. Instead of addressing concerns directly, the individual may rely on passive-aggressive behavior or cryptic hints, leading to a breakdown in open, honest communication.

Deteriorating Self-Esteem: Overthinking often leads to a decrease in self-esteem. The individual's constant self-criticism and doubts about their partner's feelings can erode their self-worth.

Breaking Free from Overthinking in Personal Relationships

While overthinking in personal relationships can be challenging, it is not an insurmountable issue. There are strategies and techniques that individuals can employ to break free from this detrimental pattern and build healthier, more fulfilling connections with their loved ones.

CHAPTER 6

GETTING RID OF OVERTHINKING
1. THE IMPACT OF BEING PRESENT

The Impact of Being Present in personal relationships is profound, fostering deeper emotional connections, reducing overthinking and anxiety, and creating a sense of genuine intimacy that enriches the quality of interactions, ultimately contributing to healthier, more fulfilling relationships.

Whether it's romantic, family, or friendship relationships, the skill of being present is a potent but sometimes underappreciated force that may change the dynamics and strengthen bonds. In a relationship, being present is putting aside distractions, giving your partner, friend, or family member your whole attention, and participating completely in the moment.

The idea is straightforward, yet it has a significant effect. We will examine the many facets of being present in intimate relationships in this thorough investigation, learning how it affects emotional bonding, lessens worry and over-analyzing, and enhances the general well-being and fulfillment of our relationships.

The Power of Being Present

Being present is a state of mind that reflects mindfulness and a commitment to the here and now. It requires us to put aside the weight of the past and the uncertainties of the future, allowing us to fully engage with the person in front of us. The impact of being present is far-reaching, and its benefits extend to multiple facets of personal relationships:

Fostering Deeper Emotional Connections

Being present is the cornerstone of deep emotional connections. It signifies that you value and prioritize the person you are with, and it creates a space for vulnerability and genuine sharing. When individuals are fully present in a relationship, they listen attentively, express empathy, and make the other person feel heard and understood. This fosters trust and emotional intimacy, making it easier to share fears, desires, and dreams. The relationship becomes a safe haven for authentic communication and connection.

Reducing Overthinking and Anxiety

Overthinking, a common nemesis in personal relationships, is often a result of dwelling on past mistakes or worrying about the future. Being present helps to quell this tendency by redirecting our focus to the present moment. When we engage fully with our loved ones, we naturally let go of anxieties about what might happen or regrets about what has already occurred. The mind is brought to a state of rest, reducing the constant cycle of overthinking that can hinder relationships.

Enhancing Communication

Communication is the lifeblood of any relationship. Being present is vital for effective and meaningful communication. It means actively listening to the words, emotions, and non-verbal cues of the other person. In doing so, we are more attuned to their needs and feelings, and we can respond with greater sensitivity. Being present enriches the quality of conversations, minimizes misunderstandings, and fosters a sense of being truly heard.

Creating a Sense of Safety

Being present in a relationship contributes to the creation of a safe and nurturing environment. When people feel that their thoughts, feelings, and experiences are respected and valued, they are more likely to open up and be themselves. This sense of safety allows individuals to express vulnerability without fear of judgment or rejection. It forms the foundation of trust, which is essential for any healthy relationship.

Reducing Conflict

Conflict is an inevitable part of personal relationships. However, being present can help navigate conflicts more effectively. When individuals are present during disagreements, they are less likely to react defensively or with aggression. Instead, they can approach conflicts with a calm and open mindset, seeking resolution rather than escalation. Being present allows for a more constructive and empathetic handling of disagreements.

Enhancing Intimacy

Intimacy is a multifaceted concept in personal relationships. It encompasses physical intimacy, emotional closeness, and a sense of being deeply connected with another person. Being present plays a pivotal role in enhancing all these facets of intimacy. Physical intimacy becomes more meaningful when both partners are fully engaged and attentive. Emotional intimacy is nurtured through genuine conversations and the sharing of innermost thoughts and feelings. Being present contributes to an overall sense of closeness and connection that goes beyond the superficial aspects of a relationship.

Boosting Well-Being

The impact of being present on personal relationships extends to individual well-being. When individuals experience deep emotional connections and reduced conflict in their relationships, they experience lower stress levels, improved mental health, and a greater overall sense of happiness. Healthy relationships, nurtured by presence, contribute to a more fulfilling and balanced life.

Building Resilience

Resilience in relationships is about the ability to weather challenges and come out stronger. Being present helps build this resilience. When individuals are connected through presence, they can face difficulties as a united front, providing each other with support and understanding. This shared strength enables the relationship to endure and grow, even in the face of adversity.

The Role of Mindfulness

A key element of being present in personal relationships is mindfulness. Mindfulness is the practice of cultivating an awareness of the present moment without judgment. It encourages us to let go of distractions, judgments, and anxieties, focusing instead on the experience at hand. This mental discipline enables individuals to be fully present in their relationships, creating a space for deeper connections and a reduction in overthinking.

PRACTICAL STRATEGIES FOR BEING PRESENT

Put Away Distractions: In an age of smartphones and constant connectivity, it's essential to set aside distractions when spending time with your loved ones. Put away your devices, turn off the TV, and create a distraction-free environment.

Active Listening: Actively listen when the other person is speaking. Avoid planning your response while they are talking and genuinely hear what they have to say. This practice fosters better understanding and emotional connections.

Practice Mindfulness: Incorporate mindfulness practices into your daily routine, such as meditation or deep breathing exercises. These techniques can help you become more aware of the present moment and reduce the grip of overthinking.

Express Gratitude: Expressing gratitude is a powerful way to be present in a relationship. It acknowledges the value of the other person and strengthens the emotional connection.

Quality Time: Allocate quality time to spend with your loved ones. Whether it's a date night, a family outing, or a heart-to-heart conversation, make sure this time is dedicated to the other person and free from distractions.

Stay Engaged: Engage fully in your interactions. Show interest, ask questions, and be responsive to the other person's needs and emotions. This demonstrates that you value the relationship.

Key Note:

In interpersonal interactions, being present may have a transforming effect that improves emotional ties, lessens worry and overanalyzing, and builds stronger, more satisfying bonds. People may foster a deeper sense of connection and provide a secure and supportive atmosphere for their loved ones to flourish by making presence a priority. Being present has a lifelong positive influence on our relationships, whether they are romantic, familial, or close friends. It improves the quality of our relationships and promotes a more contented and balanced existence.

2. COGNITIVE BEHAVIORAL

In the realm of mental health and personal development, one therapeutic approach stands out as a powerful tool for addressing a wide array of psychological challenges and promoting overall well-being: Cognitive Behavioral Therapy, often abbreviated as CBT. This multifaceted and evidence-based framework is designed to help individuals better understand their thought patterns and behaviors, enabling them to tackle issues such as anxiety, depression, and other mental health concerns. CBT equips individuals with practical techniques and strategies that empower them to take control of their mental and emotional states, fostering personal growth and resilience.

Understanding CBT

A Holistic Approach to Mental Health

Identifying Thought Patterns: CBT begins by teaching individuals to recognize their thought patterns. These patterns can be automatic, habitual ways of thinking that may be negative or unproductive. By developing awareness of these thought patterns, individuals can begin to understand how they influence their emotions and behaviors.

Challenging Negative Beliefs: One of the core principles of CBT is challenging negative beliefs and thought distortions. These beliefs often underlie conditions such as anxiety and depression. Through the therapeutic process, individuals learn to question the validity of these beliefs and develop a more balanced and constructive perspective.

Restructuring Thoughts: Once negative beliefs are identified and challenged, individuals work on restructuring their thought patterns. This involves replacing harmful or irrational thoughts with more rational, balanced ones. This process is vital for breaking the cycle of negative thinking and fostering improved mental health.

Behavioral Strategies: In addition to addressing thought patterns, CBT incorporates strategies for modifying behaviors. Individuals learn how to change their reactions and responses to specific situations. This practical aspect of CBT empowers individuals to take action and make positive changes in their lives.

Problem Solving: CBT equips individuals with problem-solving skills that are essential for coping with various life challenges. Whether it's a personal issue or a professional dilemma, these problem-solving techniques help individuals approach difficulties with greater resilience and efficacy.

Exposure Therapy: CBT also includes exposure therapy for addressing phobias, post-traumatic stress disorder, and other conditions where avoidance behaviors are prevalent. This method gradually exposes individuals to the situations or stimuli they fear, helping them build resilience and overcome their fears.

THE APPLICATIONS OF CBT

A Versatile Therapeutic Approach

CBT is a versatile approach to therapy that can be applied to a wide range of psychological conditions and life challenges:

- **Anxiety Disorders:** CBT is particularly effective in treating anxiety disorders, including generalized anxiety disorder, social anxiety disorder, and specific phobias. It helps individuals confront and manage their fears and anxieties.

- **Depression:** For individuals struggling with depression, CBT offers a structured and effective approach to addressing negative thought patterns and behaviors that often contribute to this condition.

- **Post-Traumatic Stress Disorder (PTSD):** CBT, particularly in the form of exposure therapy, is a recognized and effective treatment for individuals dealing with the aftermath of traumatic experiences.

- **Obsessive-Compulsive Disorder (OCD):** CBT, often in conjunction with exposure and response prevention (ERP), is a primary treatment for OCD. It assists individuals in managing their obsessions and compulsions.

- **Stress Management:** CBT provides individuals with practical stress management techniques, enabling them to cope with the challenges of daily life and work-related stressors.

- **Substance Abuse and Addiction:** CBT plays a critical role in addiction treatment. It helps individuals identify triggers for their addictive behaviors and develop coping strategies to maintain sobriety.

- **Eating Disorders:** For individuals with eating disorders like anorexia nervosa, bulimia, or binge-eating disorder, CBT is employed to challenge distorted body image perceptions and modify disordered eating behaviors.

- **Relationship Issues:** CBT is also applied in relationship counseling to address communication problems, conflicts, and other challenges couples may face.

- **Personal Development:** CBT is not limited to addressing mental health conditions. It can also be a valuable tool for personal growth and development. Individuals can use CBT techniques to build self-esteem, increase resilience, and achieve their personal and professional goals.

THE EVIDENCE SUPPORTING CBT

The Therapeutic Process

CBT is one of the therapy modalities with the most empirical backing because of its extensive study base. It has been shown in several trials to be useful in treating a variety of psychological problems. Because CBT is grounded on research, both individuals and mental health professionals may be confident in its effectiveness.

How CBT Works

The therapeutic process in CBT typically involves several stages:

Assessment: The therapist works with the individual to gain an understanding of their issues, symptoms, and thought patterns. This assessment provides a foundation for developing a treatment plan.

Setting Goals: Individuals, in collaboration with their therapist, set specific and achievable goals for therapy.

These goals guide the treatment process and provide a sense of direction.

Intervention: The core of CBT is the intervention phase. This is where individuals learn about their thought patterns, challenge negative beliefs, and develop practical strategies for managing their thoughts and behaviors.

Homework Assignments: Individuals are often given homework assignments to reinforce what they learn in therapy. These assignments may involve practicing techniques or monitoring their thoughts and behaviors in real-life situations.

Evaluation and Feedback: Throughout therapy, individuals and their therapists regularly evaluate progress. Feedback from the therapist helps individuals fine-tune their strategies and make necessary adjustments.

Termination and Relapse Prevention: As individuals make progress and achieve their therapy goals, therapy gradually comes to an end. However, relapse prevention strategies are often discussed to help individuals maintain the progress they've made.

THE ROLE OF THE THERAPIST

A Guide to Positive Change

In CBT, the therapist serves as a guide and collaborator on the journey to positive change. They provide support, education, and a structured framework for individuals to address their challenges and achieve their goals. The therapist's role includes:

Empathy and Understanding: Therapists create a safe and empathetic environment where individuals feel comfortable sharing their thoughts and feelings.

Education: Therapists educate individuals about their conditions and the principles of CBT, helping them understand how their thoughts and behaviors influence their mental health.

Collaboration: CBT is a collaborative process, with individuals actively participating in their treatment. Therapists work with individuals to set goals and develop strategies that work for them.

Feedback: Therapists provide feedback and guidance, helping individuals identify thought patterns, beliefs, and behaviors that may be contributing to their challenges.

Accountability: Therapists help individuals stay on track by holding them accountable for their homework assignments and progress.

Support and Encouragement: Therapists offer support and encouragement, helping individuals build resilience and confidence in their ability to make positive changes.

3. METHODS FOR COGNITIVE BEHAVIORAL STRESS REDUCTION AND UNWINDING

Techniques for Cognitive Behavioral Meditation and Relaxation encompass a diverse array of strategies that blend cognitive behavioral therapy principles with mindfulness and relaxation practices to help individuals alleviate stress, manage their emotions, and foster mental well-being, ultimately providing them with practical tools for enhancing their overall quality of life and personal growth."

Cognitive Restructuring: Cognitive restructuring is a foundational technique in CBT that can be integrated into meditation and relaxation practices. It involves identifying and challenging negative thought patterns and replacing them with more balanced and constructive thoughts. When applied to meditation, individuals can use cognitive restructuring to quiet their minds and let go of distressing or intrusive thoughts, creating a more serene mental environment.

Mindfulness Meditation: Mindfulness meditation is a well-known relaxation technique that aligns with the principles of CBT. It encourages individuals to be fully present in the moment, acknowledging their thoughts and feelings without judgment. This practice can help individuals become more aware of their automatic negative thoughts and teach them to detach from these thoughts, reducing their impact on emotional well-being.

Progressive Muscle Relaxation: Progressive muscle relaxation is a relaxation technique that involves tensing and then relaxing different muscle groups in the body. While it's primarily a relaxation practice, it can be integrated with CBT by using it to break the cycle of physical tension often associated with anxiety and stress. By reducing physical tension, individuals can experience a corresponding reduction in psychological distress.

Guided Imagery: Guided imagery is a relaxation technique that encourages individuals to create vivid mental images that promote relaxation and reduce stress. When combined with cognitive behavioral principles, individuals can use guided imagery to reframe their perceptions of stressful situations. By visualizing a more positive outcome or a calm response to stressors, they can change their emotional and behavioral reactions.

Breathing Exercises: Breathing exercises are a staple of relaxation practices and can be used in conjunction with CBT to manage anxiety and stress. These exercises can help individuals regain control over their breath, which can become shallow and rapid during moments of anxiety. By practicing deep, diaphragmatic breathing, individuals can activate their body's relaxation response and reduce the physiological symptoms of stress.

Thought Records and Journals: Thought records and journals are common tools in CBT for tracking and challenging negative thought patterns. When applied to meditation and relaxation practices, individuals can use these tools to document their thoughts during moments of stress or anxiety. This can provide insight into the triggers for these negative thoughts and help individuals develop more constructive thought patterns during relaxation exercises.

Cognitive Behavioral Sleep Strategies: Sleep is essential for overall mental well-being, and cognitive behavioral techniques can be applied to improve sleep quality. Relaxation exercises, combined with cognitive restructuring, can address insomnia and sleep-related anxiety. By cultivating a more serene mental state before bedtime, individuals can improve their ability to relax and fall asleep.

Cognitive Behavioral Self-Help Workbooks: Self-help workbooks based on CBT principles are available and offer structured exercises and techniques that individuals can use to address various psychological issues. These workbooks can include relaxation exercises, meditation practices, and thought records. Combining self-help resources with mindfulness and relaxation techniques provides individuals with a structured approach to self-improvement.

Combining CBT with Mindfulness-Based Stress Reduction (MBSR): Mindfulness-Based Stress Reduction is a program that combines mindfulness meditation with cognitive behavioral principles to reduce stress and improve overall well-being. Individuals can participate in MBSR courses or integrate MBSR techniques into their own meditation and relaxation practices. This approach can provide a comprehensive toolkit for addressing stress and emotional well-being.

Cognitive Behavioral Group Therapy: Group therapy sessions that incorporate CBT principles can offer individuals the opportunity to practice meditation and relaxation techniques in a supportive environment. Sharing experiences and progress with others can enhance the effectiveness of these practices, as well as provide a sense of community and shared growth.

Smartphone Apps and Online Resources: In the digital age, there are numerous smartphone apps and online resources that offer guided meditation, relaxation exercises, and CBT-based tools. These resources make it convenient for individuals to access and practice these techniques in their daily lives, fostering mental well-being and personal growth.

Applying CBT Techniques to Specific Challenges: While relaxation and meditation practices can be beneficial for general stress and anxiety, individuals can also tailor these techniques to address specific challenges. For example, they can use CBT principles to manage performance anxiety, social anxiety, or the stress associated with a particular phobia.

Cultivating a Personalized Toolkit: One of the strengths of combining CBT with meditation and relaxation is that individuals can create a personalized toolkit of techniques that work best for their unique needs and circumstances. Through experimentation and self-awareness, individuals can identify the practices that are most effective for them.

The Synergy of Cognitive Behavioral Meditation and Relaxation

The integration of cognitive behavioral techniques with meditation and relaxation practices offers individuals a powerful toolkit for managing stress, reducing anxiety, and enhancing their overall well-being. These techniques empower individuals to take an active role in their mental and emotional health, providing practical strategies for personal growth and resilience. Whether used in everyday life, as part of a therapy process, or in self-help contexts, the synergy of these approaches fosters a more balanced and fulfilling life.

CHAPTER 7

BUILDING RESILIENCE

1. TECHNIQUES FOR DEVELOPING MENTAL HARDINESS

"Techniques for Developing Mental Hardiness" are a set of strategies and practices designed to cultivate resilience, inner strength, and the ability to thrive in the face of adversity. These techniques encompass a range of cognitive, emotional, and behavioral tools that empower individuals to navigate life's challenges with confidence and adaptability. Let's explore these techniques in more detail:

Cognitive Restructuring: Cognitive restructuring is a fundamental technique that encourages individuals to examine and reframe their thought patterns. By identifying and challenging negative or unhelpful thoughts, individuals can develop a more resilient mindset. This technique involves questioning cognitive distortions, adopting a more balanced perspective, and fostering a sense of optimism, even in difficult circumstances.

Stress Inoculation Training: Stress inoculation training is a cognitive-behavioral technique that prepares individuals to cope with stress by teaching them various stress management skills. This technique involves exposure to mild stressors, allowing individuals to build confidence and adapt to stress in a controlled setting. As they gradually face stressors, they become better equipped to handle real-life challenges.

Emotional Regulation: Emotional regulation techniques help individuals manage their emotions effectively. These skills include recognizing and acknowledging emotions, understanding their triggers, and choosing healthy ways to express and cope with them. By developing emotional regulation, individuals can prevent emotional distress from overwhelming them and build resilience in the face of adversity.

Positive Affirmations: Positive affirmations involve using positive and constructive self-talk to counter negative beliefs and thoughts. These affirmations can boost self-esteem, foster a more optimistic outlook, and enhance self-confidence. By consistently practicing positive affirmations, individuals reinforce their mental hardiness and build a foundation of inner strength.

Mindfulness and Meditation: Mindfulness and meditation practices encourage individuals to stay present in the moment and cultivate self-awareness. These techniques help individuals detach from distressing thoughts and foster a sense of calm. By regularly practicing mindfulness and meditation, individuals can reduce stress and improve their emotional resilience.

Problem-Solving Skills: Problem-solving skills are vital for developing mental hardiness. This technique involves a systematic approach to identifying, defining, and addressing life's challenges. Individuals learn to break problems into manageable parts, consider various solutions, and take practical steps to resolve them. By becoming effective problem solvers, individuals build confidence in their ability to overcome obstacles.

Social Support and Networking: Maintaining a strong social support network is a crucial technique for enhancing mental hardiness. Interacting with supportive friends, family, or communities provides emotional reassurance, encouragement, and assistance during difficult times. Strong social connections bolster resilience and help individuals navigate adversity more effectively.

Goal Setting and Achievement: Setting and achieving goals, whether big or small, is a powerful technique for developing mental hardiness. This process involves defining clear objectives, breaking them down into manageable steps, and celebrating achievements along the way. Success in achieving goals fosters a sense of accomplishment and reinforces an individual's belief in their ability to overcome challenges.

Time Management and Stress Reduction: Effective time management techniques can help individuals reduce stress and improve their resilience. By organizing tasks, setting priorities, and managing their time efficiently, individuals can maintain a sense of control in their lives. These skills reduce the feeling of being overwhelmed and enhance mental hardiness.

Physical Health and Wellness: Physical health is closely intertwined with mental hardiness. Regular exercise, a balanced diet, and adequate sleep are essential techniques for maintaining physical and mental well-being. A healthy body supports a healthy mind and better equips individuals to cope with stress and challenges.

Post-Traumatic Growth: Post-traumatic growth is a technique that focuses on finding meaning and personal growth in the aftermath of adversity or trauma. Individuals who have experienced hardship can use this technique to transform their experiences into sources of strength, wisdom, and resilience.

Gratitude and Optimism: Practicing gratitude and fostering an optimistic outlook are techniques that can significantly boost mental hardiness. By regularly reflecting on the positive aspects of their lives and maintaining an optimistic perspective, individuals develop a buffer against the effects of stress and adversity.

Resilience-Building Workshops and Training: Resilience-building workshops and training programs offer structured approaches to developing mental hardiness. These programs teach individuals a range of skills, techniques, and strategies for enhancing their resilience, providing them with tools to thrive in challenging situations.

2. THE SIGNIFICANCE OF INTROSPECTION

Self-reflection, self-awareness, and the investigation of one's ideas, feelings, and experiences are all components of the incredibly beneficial and trans-formative process known as introspection. It is extremely important for mental health and personal growth since it is essential for developing resilience, self-awareness, and emotional control.

Through introspection, people may go on an internal trip and explore their deepest psychological corners to learn a great deal about their ideas, feelings, and actions. This procedure highlights a number of crucial facets of its significance

Enhanced Self-Awareness: Introspection serves as a mirror that reflects one's inner landscape. By taking the time to introspect, individuals can gain a clearer understanding of their beliefs, values, desires, strengths, weaknesses, and personal preferences. This heightened self-awareness empowers them to make more informed decisions and align their actions with their true selves.

Emotional Regulation: The process of introspection allows individuals to navigate their emotions more effectively. By examining the root causes of their feelings and acknowledging them without judgment, they can develop emotional intelligence. This, in turn, facilitates the management of stress, anxiety, and the ability to respond to challenging situations with composure.

Conflict Resolution: Introspection plays a crucial role in resolving interpersonal conflicts. When individuals introspect, they can better understand their own triggers, biases, and communication patterns. This self-awareness enhances their capacity to empathize with others, identify common ground, and engage in productive dialogue, ultimately promoting harmonious relationships.

Personal Growth: Introspection is a catalyst for personal growth and development. By scrutinizing their past experiences, individuals can learn from their mistakes and celebrate their achievements. This reflection enables them to set meaningful goals, strive for self-improvement, and continuously evolve as individuals.

Resilience: Introspection contributes to mental resilience. When individuals explore their reactions to adversity and setbacks, they can identify coping mechanisms and develop a more positive mindset. This resilience helps them bounce back from challenges with greater strength and adaptability.

Enhanced Decision-Making: A significant benefit of introspection is its influence on decision-making. By carefully examining their values and priorities, individuals can make choices that align with their authentic selves. They become more adept at making informed decisions that lead to greater satisfaction and fulfillment.

Stress Reduction: Introspection serves as a stress management tool. It allows individuals to identify the sources of stress in their lives and explore their internal responses to these stressors. This awareness paves the way for effective stress reduction strategies, such as mindfulness, relaxation techniques, and problem-solving.

Improved Communication: Effective communication is a hallmark of introspection. By understanding their own communication patterns, individuals can adapt their style to be more empathetic and clear in their interactions with others. This results in more meaningful and productive conversations.

Empathy and Compassion: Introspection nurtures empathy and compassion for oneself and others. By reflecting on their own experiences, individuals can relate to the struggles and joys of others. This deepened empathy fosters compassion, leading to more meaningful and supportive relationships.

Enhanced Creativity: The introspective process often leads to creative insights. As individuals reflect on their thoughts and experiences, they may discover innovative solutions to challenges, novel perspectives, and creative ideas that can benefit various aspects of their lives.

Spiritual and Existential Exploration: For many, introspection becomes a tool for spiritual and existential exploration. It encourages individuals to contemplate life's meaning, their purpose, and their connection to the broader universe. This deep introspection can be profoundly transformative, leading to spiritual growth and a sense of inner peace.

Key note:

The process of reflection has many facets and is crucial to one's wellbeing and personal growth. It gives people the ability to delve into their inner selves, become more self-aware, improve emotional control, and become resilient. People who engage in reflection are better able to communicate, make well-informed judgments, and develop understanding and compassion. Personal development, creativity, and even spiritual investigation are aided by this process. Introspection is an important technique for self-improvement and self-discovery on the path to a deeper sense of fulfillment and self-awareness.

THE VALUE OF A SUPPORT SYSTEM

"The Value of a Support System" is a fundamental aspect of personal well-being and mental resilience. It centers around the recognition and appreciation of the positive influence and contributions of a support system in an individual's life, as well as the critical role it plays in fostering emotional strength and psychological health. The significance of this point encompasses several key dimensions:

Emotional Support: A support system provides a safe and empathetic space for individuals to express their feelings and concerns. This emotional support enables them to share their joys and sorrows, navigate difficult times, and experience a sense of validation and understanding.

Stress Reduction: The presence of a support system can significantly alleviate stress and anxiety. Being able to confide in trusted friends, family, or individuals within the support network can help in reducing the emotional burden that accompanies challenging situations.

Resilience and Coping: Support systems bolster an individual's capacity to cope with adversity. Whether facing personal setbacks or larger life challenges, knowing that they have people to turn to for guidance and encouragement fosters resilience and helps them bounce back from difficulties.

Validation and Empathy: Support systems offer validation and empathy, allowing individuals to feel heard and understood. This validation reinforces their self-worth and encourages them to process their emotions, ultimately promoting a sense of emotional well-being.

Problem-Solving and Perspective: Trusted individuals in a support system often provide fresh perspectives and guidance. They can help in problem-solving, offering alternative viewpoints and solutions that individuals may not have considered on their own.

Enhanced Communication: Having a support system nurtures effective communication skills. Individuals learn to express themselves clearly and honestly, fostering healthier and more meaningful relationships.

Reduced Isolation: One of the most significant aspects of a support system is that it combats isolation. Isolation can lead to feelings of loneliness and depression. Knowing that there are people who care and are available can be a powerful antidote to these feelings.

Mental Health and Well-Being: The presence of a support system is closely linked to improved mental health. It can provide a buffer against conditions such as depression and anxiety. Supportive relationships often lead to increased life satisfaction and happiness.

Positive Influence: A support system often consists of individuals who have a positive influence on an individual's life. They can motivate, inspire, and encourage personal growth and self-improvement.

Building Trust: Being part of a support system is an opportunity to build and strengthen trust in relationships. Trust is a foundational element of meaningful connections.

Social Engagement: A support system can encourage and facilitate social engagement and participation in various activities, enriching an individual's life and helping them build a sense of belonging within a community.

Healthy Relationships: Learning how to navigate and maintain healthy relationships is a valuable life skill. Support systems contribute to this learning process by providing an environment for practicing effective communication and conflict resolution.

Key note:

"The Value of a Support System" emphasizes how important it is for someone to have a network of reliable people in their life. It helps to reduce stress, promote resilience, and provide emotional support. A support network improves mental health, lessens feelings of loneliness and isolation, and encourages honest and compassionate communication. Support networks improve people's lives by fostering constructive relationships and the development of trust, which promotes personal development and deep connections. A support network encompasses almost every facet of a person's happiness and well-being, making it an invaluable asset.

CHAPTER 8

CONCLUSION

We have examined the wide-ranging effects of overthinking in this book and offered a thorough insight and solution to this frequent problem. Now that you have the right tools, you can reclaim your mental and personal autonomy and escape the shackles of overthinking. Applying the techniques and ideas found in this book will enable you to look forward to a day when mental clarity, self-assurance, and tranquility are the rule rather than the exception.

111